MARRIAGE & LOVE

To buy books in quantity for corporate use
or incentives, call **(800) 962–0973**
or e-mail **premiums@GlobePequot.com**.

Lyons Press is an imprint of Globe Pequot Press.

Text design and layout: Georgiana Goodwin

Project editor: Kristen Mellitt

Library of Congress Cataloging-in-Publication Data
is available on file.

ISBN 978-0-7627-6390-0

Printed in the United States of America

10 9 8 7 6 5 4 3 2 1

Real Advice from 1894

MARRIAGE & LOVE

Instructions for Females on
Courtship and Matrimony,
with Tips to Discourage
Sexual Advances from Husbands

Ruth Smythers

Lyons Press
Guilford, Connecticut

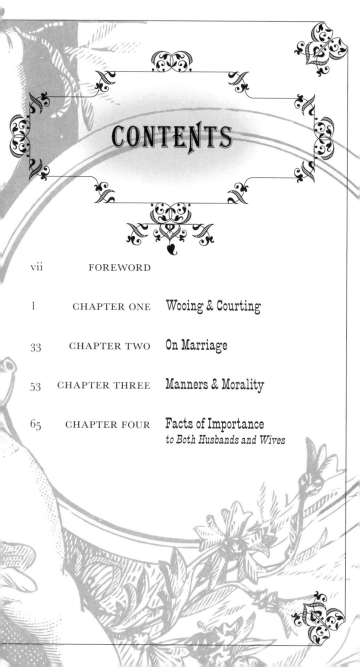

CONTENTS

FOREWORD

In just the fashion that the Underworld of Dante is brightly brought to knowledge by his guide, the glorious heathen Virgil, so, too, this tidy volume, although penned by a female, the Mistress Ruth Smythers, good wife unto the Rev. L. D. Smythers, manages in its distaff way to dig just deeply enough into the lurid netherworld of modern society's repellent preoccupation with all matters of a sportingly procreative nature (e.g., The Secret Sin so depravedly perpetrated by sensualists and profligates of both the sexes; the coarse musical theatre; public lounging; the reading of Novels; and the immoderate liberties taken even within the sacrament of marriage), as to give unto the chaste among us a frightening sense of where our hedonistic and sybaritic society might find itself even before the looming new century unfolds, unless, withal, the enlightened reader takes heed of the warning, and chooses instead to follow the practical and moral advices contained herein.

The Rev. Cornwalis J. L. G. Cilpopper, DSO, MVO, OB Hideminster Cottage, Clyburn on Wye

If you court at all, court scientifically. Bungle whatever else you will, but do not bungle courtship. A failure in this may mean more than a loss of wealth or public honors; it may mean ruin, or a life often worse than death. The world is full of wretched and mismated people.

WOOING & COURTING

Nearly all this widespread crime and suffering connected with public and private licentiousness and prostitution has its origin in unmeaning courtships—and every young man who courts without intending to marry is throwing himself or his sweetheart into this hell upon Earth.

Establish an Appropriate Appearance for Wooing

FOR SCRAWNY NECK.
Wash neck and chest with hot water, then rub in sweet oil all that you can work in. Apply this every night before you retire, and leave the skin damp while you sleep.

FOR RED HANDS.
Rub your hands with the skin of a lemon and it will whiten them.

NECK AND FACE.
Do not bathe the neck and face just before or after being out of doors. It tends to wrinkle the skin.

SCOWLS.
Never allow yourself to scowl, even if the sun be in your eyes. That scowl will soon leave its trace, and no beauty will outlive it.

WRINKLED FOREHEAD.
If you wrinkle your forehead when you talk or read, visit an oculist and have your eyes tested.

OLD LOOKS.

Sometimes your face looks old because it is tired. The following wash will make you look younger: three drops of ammonia, a little borax, a tablespoonful of bay rum, and a few drops of camphor into warm water and applied to your face. Avoid getting it into your eyes.

SPOTS ON THE FACE.

Moles and many other discolorations may be removed from the face by a preparation composed of one part chemically pure carbolic acid and two parts pure glycerine. Touch the spots with a camel's-hair pencil. Five minutes after touching, bathe with soft water and apply a little Vaseline. The operation, repeated, will entirely remove the blemishes.

WRINKLES.

This prescription is said to cure wrinkles: Take one ounce of white wax and melt it to a gentle heat. Add two ounces of the juice of lily bulbs, two ounces of honey, two drams of rose water, and a drop or two of attar of roses. Apply twice a day, rubbing the wrinkles the wrong way. Always use tepid water for washing the face.

THE HAIR.

The hair must be kept free from dust or it will fall out. One of the best things for cleaning it is a raw egg rubbed into the roots and then washed out in several waters. The egg furnishes material for the hair to grow on.

Be Not Deceived by the Flirt

Who is the flirt? What is his reputation, motive, or character?

Every young man and woman must have a reputation; if it is not good, it is bad; there is no middle ground. Young people who are running in the streets after dark, boisterous and noisy in their conversation, gossiping and giggling, flirting with first one and then another, will soon settle their matrimonial prospects among good society. Modesty is a priceless jewel. No sensible young man with a future will marry a flirt.

An infallible sign that a young man's intentions are improper is his trying to excite your passions. And the woman who allows a man to take advantage of her just to compel him to marry her is utterly destitute of moral principle as well as virtue. A woman's riches are her virtue; that gone, she has lost all.

Our cemeteries receive within the cold shadows of the grave thousands and thousands of victims who annually die from the results of "broken hearts." It is no doubt a fact that love

troubles cause more disorders of the heart than everything else combined.

The punishment of the seducer is best given by O. S. Fowler, in his *Creative and Sexual Science:* The sin and punishment rest on all you who call out only to blight a trusting, innocent, loving virgin's affections, and then discard her. You deserve to be horsewhipped by her father, cowhided by her brothers, branded villain by her mother, cursed by herself, and sent to the whipping post and dungeon.

A young lady should never encourage the attentions of a young man who shows no interest in his sisters. If a young man is indifferent to his sisters, he will become indifferent to his wife as soon as the honeymoon is over. There are few, if any, exceptions to this rule.

OLD LOOKS

Sometimes your face looks old
because it is tired. The following wash
will make you look younger:
three drops of ammonia, a little borax,
a tablespoonful of bay rum,
and a few drops of camphor into
warm water, and applied to your face.

Avoid getting it into your eyes.

What Women Love, or Disparage, in Men

Women naturally love courage, force, and firmness in men. The ideal man in a woman's eye must be heroic and brave. Woman naturally despises a coward, and she has little or no respect for a bashful man.

Woman naturally loves her lord and master. Women who desperately object to be overruled nevertheless admire men who overrule them, and few women would have any respect for a man whom they could completely rule and control.

Women naturally love men of strength, size, and fine physique, a tall, large, and strong man rather than a short, small, and weak man. A woman always pities a weakly man, but rarely ever has any love for him.

Woman never can love a man whose conversation is flat and insipid. Every man seeking woman's appreciation or love should always endeavor to show his intelligence and manifest an interest in books and daily papers. He should read books and inform himself so that he can talk intelligently upon the various topics of the day. Even an ignorant woman always loves superior intelligence.

Weakly and delicate fathers have weak and puny children, though the mother may be strong and robust. A weak mother often bears strong children, if the father is physically and sexually vigorous.

 Homely men are admired by women if they are large, strong, and vigorous and possess a good degree of intelligence. Looks are trifles compared with the other qualities which man may possess.

Woman despises a man who has no opinion of his own; she hates a trifling disposition and admires leadership and original ideas and looks up to man as a leader. Women despise all men whom they can manage, overrule, cow down, and subdue.

It is a well-known fact that women love uniformed men. The soldier figures as a hero in about every tale of fiction, and it is said by good authority that a man in uniform has three more chances to marry than the man without uniform. The correct reason is, the soldier's profession is bravery, and he is dressed and trained for that purpose, and it is that which makes him admired by ladies rather than the uniform which he wears. His profession is also that of a protector.

What Men Love (or Not) in Women

Man's love of female beauty surpasses all other love, and whatever artificial means are used to beautify, to a certain extent, are falsehoods which lead to distrust or dislike. Artificial beauty is always an imitation and never can come into competition with the genuine.

Good looks and good and pure conduct awaken a man's love for women. A girl must therefore be charming as well as beautiful, for a charming girl will never become a charmless wife.

A round, plump figure with an overflow of animal life is the woman most commonly sought, for nature in man craves for the strong qualities in women, as the health and life of offspring depend upon the physical qualities of wife and mother.

A woman with a large pelvis gives her a superior and significant appearance, while a narrow pelvis always indicates weak sexuality. The other portions of the body, however, must be in harmony with the size and breadth of the hips.

Avoiding Idiocy and Other Malformations

If marriage is delayed too long in either sex, say from thirty to forty-five, the offspring will often be puny and more liable to insanity, idiocy, and other maladies. In choosing a husband, marrying first cousins is dangerous to offspring. The observation is universal—the children of married first cousins are too often idiots, insane, clump-footed, crippled, blind, or variously diseased. First cousins are always sure to impart all the hereditary disease in both families to their children. If both are healthy there is less danger.

In the female beauty of physical development there is nothing that can equal full breasts.

It is an indication of good health and good maternal qualities. Cotton and all other false forms simply show the value of natural ones. All false forms are easily detected, because large natural ones will generally quiver and move at every step, while the artificial ones will manifest no expression of life.

Small feet and ankles indicate modesty and reserve, while large feet and ankles indicate coarseness, physical power, authority, and predominance. Feet and ankles, however, must be in harmony with the body, as small feet and small ankles on a large woman would be out of proportion and consequently not beautiful.

Men love reserved, coy, and discreet women much more than blunt, shrewd, and boisterous women. Falsehood, false hair, false curls, false forms, false bosoms, false colors, false cheeks, and all that is false, men naturally dislike, for in themselves they are a poor foundation on which to form family ties. Consequently, duplicity and hypocrisy in women are very much disliked by men, but a frank, honest, conscientious soul is always lovable and lovely and a woman with these traits will not become an old maid, except as a matter of choice and not of necessity.

Let Science Guide You in Choosing Your Mate

Bright red hair should marry jet black, jet black auburn, or bright red, etc. And the more red-faced and bearded or impulsive a man, the more dark, calm, cool, and quiet should his wife be; and vice versa.

The florid should not marry the florid but those who are dark, in proportion as they themselves are light.

Red-whiskered men should marry brunettes, but no blondes—the color of the whiskers being more determinate of the temperament than that of the hair.

Gray eyes must marry almost any other except gray; and so of blue, dark, hazel, etc.

Those very fleshy should not marry those equally so, but those spare and slim. A spare man is much better adapted to a fleshy woman than a round-favored man.

Two who are short, thickset, and stocky should not unite in marriage, but should choose those differently constituted.

Those with little hair or beard should marry those whose hair is naturally abundant; still those who once had plenty, but who have lost it, may marry those who are either bald or have but little.

Those who are bony, only moderately fleshy, quite prominent featured, Roman nosed, and muscular should not marry those similarly formed.

Small, nervous men must not marry little, nervous, or sanguine women, lest both they and their children have quite too much of the hotheaded and impulsive, and die suddenly.

Two very beautiful persons rarely do or should marry, nor two extra homely. The fact is a little singular that very handsome women, who of course can have their pick, rarely marry good-looking men, but generally give preference to those who are homely.

Noses indicate characters by indicating the organisms and temperaments. Accordingly, those noses especially marked either way should marry those having opposite nasal characteristics. Roman noses are adapted to those which turn up, pug noses to those turning down, while straight noses may marry either.

A timid woman should never marry a hesitating man, lest, like frightened children, each keep perpetually re-alarming the other by imaginary fears.

Rapid movers, speakers, laughers, etc., should marry those who are calm and deliberate, and impulsives should marry those who are stoical. Those who are medium may marry those who are either or neither, as they prefer.

Marrying small waists is attended with consequences scarcely less disastrous than marrying rich and fashionable girls. Small waists indicate small and feeble vital organs, a delicate constitution, sickly offspring, and a short life. Beware of them, therefore, unless you wish your heart broken by the early death of your wife and children.

Do not marry a man with a low, flat head; for, however fascinating, genteel, polite, tender,  plausible, or winning he may be, you will repent the day of your espousal.

A small stature is objectionable in a woman, because little women usually have too much activity for their strength, and, consequently, feeble constitutions; hence they die young, and besides, being nervous, suffer extremely as mothers.

Men who love to command must be especially careful not to marry imperious, women's-rights women; while those who willingly "obey orders" need just such. Some men require a wife who shall take their part; yet all who do not need strong-willed women, should be careful how they marry them.

Confronting the Evils of Sensuality

This is an age of sensuality; unnatural passions cultivated and indulged. Young people in the course of their engagement often sow the seed of serious excesses. This habit of embracing, sitting on the lover's lap, leaning on his breast, and long and uninterrupted periods of secluded companionship, have become so common that it is amazing how a young lady can safely arrive at the wedding day.

The church should turn its face like flint against the public ball or dance. Its influence is evil, and nothing but evil. It is a well-known fact that in all cities and large towns the ballroom is the recruiting office for prostitution.

Thoughtless Young Women

In cities, public balls are given every night, and many thoughtless young women, mostly  the daughters of small tradesmen and mechanics or clerks or laborers, are induced to attend "just for fun." Scarcely one in a hundred of the girls attending these balls preserves her purity. They meet the most desperate characters, professional gamblers, criminals, and the lowest debauchees. Such an assembly and such influence cannot mean anything but ruin for an innocent girl.

The low theater and dance halls and other places of unselected gatherings are the milestones which mark the working girl's downward path from virtue to vice, from modesty to shame.

There is not a young girl but what is more or less tempted by some unprincipled wretch who may have the reputation of a genteel society man. It behooves parents to guard carefully the morals of their daughters and be vigilant and cautious in permitting them to accept the society of young men.

Parents who desire to save their daughters from a fate which is worse than death should endeavor by every means in their power to keep them from falling into traps cunningly devised by some cunning lover. There are many good young men, but not all are safe friends to an innocent, confiding young girl.

An infallible sign that a
young man's intentions are improper,
is his trying to excite your passions.
And the woman who allows a man
to take advantage
of her just to compel him to marry
her, is utterly destitute of moral
principle as well as virtue.

The dance, the theater, the wine cup, the racecourse, the idle frivolity and luxury of summer watering places—all have a tendency to demoralize the young.

The low theater and dance halls and other places of unselected gatherings are the milestones which mark the working girl's downward path from virtue to vice, from modesty to shame.

Toward Being a Wife

All are born with the desire to become attractive—girls especially want to grow up not only attractive, but beautiful. Some girls think that bright eyes, pretty hair, and fine clothes alone make them beautiful. This is not so. Real beauty depends upon good health, good manners, and a pure mind.

All women cannot have good features, but they can look well, and it is possible to a great extent to correct deformity and develop much of the figure. The first step to good looks is good health, and the first element of health is cleanliness. Keep clean—wash freely, bathe regularly. All the skin wants is leave to act, and it takes care of itself.

Do not get the idea that men admire a weakly, puny, delicate, small-waisted, languid, doll-like creature, a libel on true womanhood. Girls admire men with broad chests, square shoulders, erect form, keen bright eyes, hard muscles, and undoubted vigor. Men also turn naturally to healthy, robust, well-developed girls, and to win their admiration girls must meet their ideals.

A woman five feet tall should measure two feet around the waist and thirty-three inches around the hips. A waist less than this proportion indicates compression either by lacing or tight clothing. Exercise in the open air, take long walks and vigorous exercise, using care not to overdo it. Housework will prove a panacea for many of the ills which flesh is heir to. One hour's exercise at the washtub is of far more value, from a physical standpoint, than hours at the piano. Boating is most excellent exercise and within the reach of many.

Care in dressing is also important, and, fortunately, fashion is coming to the rescue here. It is essential that no garments be suspended from the waist. Let the shoulders bear the

weight of all the clothing so that the organs of the body may be left free and unimpeded.

If the hands are allowed to swing in walking, the arc should be limited, and the lady will manage them much more gracefully if they almost touch the clothing.

A lady should not stand with her hands behind her. We could almost say, forget the hands except to keep them clean, including the nails, cordial, and helpful. One hand may rest easily in the other. Study repose of attitude here as well as in the rest of the body.

Greet your acquaintances as you meet them with a slight bow and smile, as you speak. Look the person to whom you speak in the eye. Never under any circumstances wink at another or communicate by furtive looks.

A true lady will avoid familiarity in her deportment toward gentlemen. A young lady should not permit her gentlemen friends to address her by her home name, and the reverse is true. Use the titles Miss and Mr. respectively.

If a young lady desires to visit any public place where she expects to meet a gentleman acquaintance, she should have a chaperone to accompany her, a person of mature years when possible and never a giddy girl.

The mother who has ruined her health by late hours, highly-spiced food, and general carelessness in regard to hygienic laws, and the father who is the slave of questionable habits, will be very sure to have children either mentally or morally inferior to what they might otherwise have had a right to expect.

Don'ts: How *Not* to Behave

Don't pick the nose, finger about the ears, or scratch the head or any other part of the person in company; it is decidedly vulgar.

Don't let one day pass without a thorough cleansing of your person.

Don't sit down to your evening meal before a complete toilet if you have company.

Don't cleanse your nails, your nose, or your ears in public.

Don't use hair dye, hair oil, or pomades.

Don't wear evening dress in daytime.

Don't wear jewelry of a gaudy character; genuine jewelry modestly worn is not out of place.

Don't overdress yourself or walk affectedly.

Don't wear slippers or a dressing gown or smoking jacket out of your own house.

Don't sink your hands in your trousers' pockets.

Don't whistle in public places, nor inside of houses either.

Don't use your fingers or fists to beat a tattoo upon floor, desk, or windowpanes.

Don't examine other people's papers or letters scattered on their desk.

Don't bring a smell of spirits or tobacco into the presence of ladies; never use either in the presence of ladies.

Don't drink spirits; millions have tried it to their sorrow.

Marriage has proven itself to be a tonic for the husband and for the wife. Reciprocated love produces a general exhilaration of the system. The elasticity of the muscles is increased, the circulation is quickened, and every bodily function is stimulated to renewed activity by a happy marriage.

ON MARRIAGE

Marriage is a sure and specific remedy for all the ills known as seminal losses. As right eating cures a sick stomach and right breathing diseased lungs, so the right use of the sexual organs will bring relief and restoration.

Many men who have been sufferers from indiscretions of youth have married and were soon cured of spermatorrhoea and other complications which accompanied it.

Some Fundamental Observations on the Estate of Marriage

The lady should select the wedding day. There is one element in the time that is of great importance, physically, especially to the lady.

It is the day of the month, and it is hoped that every lady who contemplates marriage is informed upon the great facts of ovulation.

It is to her advantage to select a wedding day
about fifteen or eighteen days after the close
of menstruation in the month chosen, since
it is not best that the first child should be
conceived during the excitement or irritation
of first attempts at congress; besides modest
brides naturally do not wish to become large
with child before the season of congratula-
tion and visiting on their return from the
"wedding tour" is over.

On Making a Good Wife

The good husband will allow his life companion a bank account, and will exact no itemized bill at the end of the month. Above all, he will pay the Easter bonnet bill without a word. So after all, good husbands have the most to do with making good wives.

To be the best homemaker, a woman needs to be devoid of intensive "nerves." She should have no "career," or desire for a career, if she would fill to perfection the home sphere.

Women too early married always remain small in stature, weak, pale, emaciated, and more or less miserable.

Now, if a woman cannot broil a beefsteak, nor boil the coffee when it is necessary; if she cannot mend the linen, nor patch a coat; if she cannot make a bed, order the dinner, create a lampshade, ventilate the house, nor do anything practical in the way of making home actually a home, how can she expect to make even a good wife, not to speak of a better or best wife?

On Being a Young Husband

The great majority of men experience frequent strong sexual desire. Abstention is very apt to produce in their minds voluptuous images and untamable desires which require an iron will to banish or control. Men who inherit strong passions easily argue themselves into the belief either to practice masturbation or visit places of prostitution, on the ground that their health demands it.

Though medical investigation has proven it repeatedly to be false, yet many believe it. Masturbation or prostitution soon blight the brightest prospects a young man may have. Manhood is morality and purity of purpose, not sensuality.

Many a young husband often lays the foundation of many diseases of the womb and of the nervous system in gratifying his unchecked passions without a proper regard for his wife's exhausted condition.

Wives Pay Heed

No wife should indulge her husband when he is under the influence of alcoholic stimulants, for idiocy and other serious maladies are liable to be visited upon the offspring.

As long as children are the accidents of lust instead of the premeditated objects of love, so long will the offspring deteriorate and the world be cursed with deformities, monstrosities, unhumanities, and cranks.

For a certain period between her monthly illness, every woman is sterile. Conception may be avoided by refraining from coition except for this particular number of days, and there will be no evasion of natural intercourse, no resort to disgusting practices, and nothing degrading.

If the parties of a marriage are both feeble and so adapted to each other that their children are deformed, insane, or idiots, then to beget offspring would be a flagrant wrong.

Selden H. Tascott says: "Ungoverned passions in the parents may unloose the furies of unrestrained madness in the minds of

38

their children. Many causes have operated to produce a corruption of the public morals so deplorable; prominent among which may be mentioned the facility with which divorces may be obtained in some of the States, the constant promulgation of false ideas of marriage and its duties by means of books, lectures, etc., and the distribution through the mails of impure publications."

It is known that the girl who marries the man with bad habits, is, in a measure, responsible for the evil tendencies which these habits have created in the children. The mother who has ruined her health by late hours, highly spiced food, and general carelessness in regard to hygienic laws, and the father who is the slave of questionable habits, will be very sure to have children either mentally or morally inferior to what they might otherwise have had a right to expect.

Withstanding the Ordeal of Procreation

It is asserted by many of the best writers on this subject that the mental condition of either parent at the time of intercourse will be stamped upon the embryo, hence it is not only best, but wise, that the firstborn should not be conceived until several months after marriage, when the husband and wife have nicely settled in their new home and become calm in their experience of each other's society.

To the sensitive young woman who has had the benefits of proper upbringing, the wedding day is, ironically, both the happiest and most terrifying day of her life. On the positive side, there is the wedding itself, in which the bride is the central attraction in a beautiful and inspiring ceremony, symbolizing her triumph in securing a male to provide for all her needs for the rest of her life. On the negative side, there is the wedding night, during which the bride must pay the piper, so to speak, by facing for the first time the terrible experience of sex.

At this point, dear reader, let me concede one shocking truth. Some young women actually anticipate the wedding night ordeal with curiosity and pleasure! Beware such an attitude! A selfish and sensual husband can easily take advantage of such a bride.

It is useless, in most cases, for the bride to prevail upon the groom to forego the sexual initiation. While the ideal husband would be one who would approach his bride only at her request and only for the purpose of begetting offspring, such nobility and unselfishness cannot be expected from the average man.

One cardinal rule of marriage should never be forgotten:

Give little, give seldom, and above all, give grudgingly.

Otherwise what could have been a proper marriage could become an orgy of sexual lust.

While sex is at best revolting and at worse rather painful, it has to be endured, and has been by women since the beginning of time, and is compensated for by the monogamous home and by the children produced through it.

Dr. Dio Lewis says: "Occasionally we meet a diseased female with excessive animal passion, but such a case is very rare. The average woman has so little sexual desire that if licentiousness depended upon her, uninfluenced by her desire to please man or secure his support, there would be very little sexual excess."

Most men, if not denied, would demand sex almost every day. The wise bride will permit a maximum of two brief sexual experiences weekly during the first months of marriage. As time goes by she should make every effort to reduce this frequency.

Feigned illness, sleepiness, and headaches are among the wife's best friends in this matter. Arguments, nagging, scolding, and bickering also prove very effective, if used in the late evening about an hour before the husband would normally commence his seduction.

By their tenth anniversary many wives have managed to complete their childbearing and have achieved the ultimate goal of terminating all sexual contacts with the husband.

Just as she should be ever alert to keep the quantity of sex as low as possible, the wise bride will pay equal attention to limiting the kind and degree of sexual contacts.

Most men are by nature rather perverted, and if given half a chance, would engage in quite a variety of the most revolting practices. These practices include among others performing the normal act in abnormal positions; mouthing the female body; and offering their own vile bodies to be mouthed in turn.

Nudity, talking about sex, reading stories about sex, and viewing photographs and drawings depicting or suggesting sex are the obnoxious habits the male is likely to acquire if permitted.

A wise bride will make it her goal never to allow her husband to see her unclothed body, and never allow him to display his unclothed body to her.

Sex, when it cannot be prevented, should be practiced only in total darkness.

Many women have found it useful to have thick cotton nightgowns for themselves and pajamas for their husbands. These should be donned in separate rooms. They need not be removed during the sex act. Thus, a minimum of flesh is exposed.

Once the bride has donned her gown and turned off all the lights, she should lie quietly upon the bed and await her groom. When he comes groping into the room she should make no sound to guide him in her direction, lest he take this as a sign of encouragement.

The bride should let her groom grope for her  in the dark. There is always the hope that he will stumble and incur some slight injury which she can use as an excuse to deny him sexual access.

When the groom finds the bride within the darkened bedchamber, the wife should lie as still as possible. Bodily motion on her part could be interpreted as sexual excitement by the optimistic husband.

If he attempts to kiss her on the lips, she should turn her head slightly so that the kiss falls harmlessly on her cheek instead.

If he attempts to kiss her hand, she should make a fist.

If he lifts her gown and attempts to kiss her anyplace else, she should quickly pull the gown back in place, spring from the bed, and announce that nature calls her to the toilet. This will generally dampen his desire to kiss in the forbidden territory.

If the husband attempts to seduce her with lascivious talk, the wise wife will suddenly remember some trivial nonsexual question to ask him. Once he answers she should keep the conversation going, no matter how frivolous it may seem at the time.

Eventually the husband will learn that if he insists on having sexual contact, he must get on with it without amorous embellishment.

The wise wife will allow him to pull the gown up no farther than the waist, and only permit

him to open the front of his pajamas to thus make connection.

During the repulsive act, the wife should be absolutely silent or babble about her housework while he is huffing and puffing away. Above all, she should lie perfectly still and never under any circumstances grunt or groan while the act is in progress.

As soon as the husband has completed the act, the wise wife will start nagging him about various minor tasks she wishes him to perform on the morrow.

Many men obtain a major portion of their sexual satisfaction from the peaceful exhaustion immediately after the filthy act is over. Thus the wife must insure that there is no peace in this period for him to enjoy. Otherwise, he might be encouraged to soon try for more.

One heartening factor for which the wife can be grateful is the fact that the husband's home, school, church, and social environment have been working together all through his

life to instill in him a deep sense of guilt in regards to his sexual feelings, so that he comes to the marriage couch apologetically and filled with shame, already half-cowed and subdued. The wise wife seizes upon this advantage and relentlessly pursues her goal first to limit, later to annihilate completely, her husband's desire for sexual expression.

The Dour Effects of Sexual Indulgence

Most men of the educated classes enter the marriage bed with the consciousness of leaving behind them a whole army of prostitutes or seduced women, in whose arms they cooled their passions and spent the vigor of their youth.

With such a past the married man does not at the same time leave behind him its influence on his inclinations. The habit of having a feminine being at his disposal for every rising appetite, and the desire for change inordinately indulged for years, generally make themselves felt again as soon as the honeymoon is over.

Marriage will not make a morally corrupt man all at once a good man and a model husband.

Nor are many persons sufficiently aware of the ruinous extent to which the amative propensity is indulged by married persons.

The matrimonial ceremony does, indeed, sanctify the act of sexual intercourse, but it can by no means atone for nor obviate the consequences of its abuse. Excessive indulgence in the married relation is, perhaps, as much owing to the force of habit, as to the force of the sexual appetite.

Furthermore, every sexual excitement is exhaustive in proportion to its intensity and continuance. If a man sits by the side of a woman, fondles and kisses her for three or four hours, and allows his imagination to run riot with sexual visions, he will be five times as much exhausted as he would by the act culminating in emission.

So, wives, be exceedingly careful of license and excess in your intercourse with your husband. Do not needlessly expose, by undress, the body. Let not the purity of love degenerate into unholy lust! See to it that you walk according to the divine Word. "Dwelling together as being heirs of the grace of life, that your prayers be not hindered."

Just as she should be ever alert
to keep the quantity of sex as low
as possible, the wise bride will pay
equal attention to limiting the kind
and degree of sexual contacts.

It is a fact well answered by statistics that there is more crime committed, more vices practiced, and more immorality among single men than among married men. The vices of single men support the most flagrant of evils of modern society, hence let every young man beware and keep his body clean and pure. His future happiness largely depends upon his chastity while a single man.

The indulgence of illicit pleasures, says Dr. S. Pancoast, is sure to entail the most loathsome diseases. Among these diseases are gonorrhoea, syphilis, spermatorrhoea (waste of semen by daily and nightly involuntary emissions), satyriasis (a species of sexual madness, or a sexual diabolism, causing men to commit rape and other beastly acts and outrages, not only on women and children, but men and animals, as sodomy, pederasty, etc.).

MANNERS & MORALITY

Yet another dreadful, yet, often unavoidable outcome of immoderate pleasure seeking is nymphomania (causing women to assail every man they meet, and supplicate and excite him to gratify their lustful passions, or who resort to means of sexual pollutions, which is impossible to describe without shuddering), together with spinal diseases and many disorders of the most distressing and disgusting character filling the bones with rottenness and eating away the flesh by gangrenous ulcers, until the patient dies, a horrible mass of putridity and corruption.

Self-Pollution at the Heart of Many Moral and Physical Failures

When the male organ comes in contact with female magnetism, the natural and proper excitement takes place. When excited *without this female magnetism* it becomes one of the most serious injuries to the human body.

The male organ was made for a high and holy purpose, and woe be to him who pollutes his manhood by practicing the secret vice. He pays the penalty in after years either by the entire loss of sexual power, or by the afflictions of various urinary diseases. Nature pays all her debts, and when there is an abuse of organ, penalties must follow. If the hand is thrust into the fire, it will be burnt.

There is one way of destroying health, which, fortunately, is not as common among girls as boys, and which must be mentioned ere this chapter closes. Self-abuse is practiced among growing girls to such an extent as to arouse serious alarm.

Many a girl has been led to handle and play
with her sexual organs through the advice
of some girl who has obtained temporary
pleasure in that way; or, perchance, chafing
has been followed by rubbing until the organs
have become congested with blood, and in
this accidental manner the girl discovered
what seems to her a source of pleasure, but
which, alas, is a source of misery, and even
death.

In the boy, so in the girl, self-abuse causes
an undue amount of blood to flow to those
organs, thus depriving other parts of the body
of its nourishment, the weakest part first show-
ing the effect of want of sustenance.

All that has been said upon this loathsome subject might well be repeated here, but space forbids. Know that the same signs that betray the boy will make known the girl addicted to the vice.

The bloodless lips; the dull, heavy eye surrounded with dark rings; the nerveless hand; the blanched cheek; the short breath; the old, faded look; the weakened memory and silly irritability tell the story all too plainly.

The same evil result follows, ending perhaps in death, or worse, in insanity. Aside from the injury the girl does herself by yielding to this habit, there is one other reason that appeals to the conscience, and that is, self-abuse is an offense against moral law—it is putting to a vile, selfish use the organs which were given for a high, sacred purpose.

If the sexual organs are handled, it brings too much blood to these parts, and this produces a diseased condition; it also causes disease in other organs of the body, because they are left with a less amount of blood than they ought to have. The sexual organs, too, are very closely connected with the spine and the brain by means of the nerves, and if they are handled, or if you keep thinking about them, these nerves get excited and become exhausted, and this makes the back ache, the brain heavy, and the whole body weak.

It lays the foundation for consumption, paralysis, and heart disease. It weakens the memory, makes a boy careless, negligent, and listless. It even makes many lose their minds; others, when grown, commit suicide. How often mothers see their little boys handling themselves, and let it pass, because they think the boy will outgrow the habit, and do not realize the strong hold it has upon them. I say to you who love your boys—"Watch!"

Many Are the Evils to Which Flesh Is Prey

On the Hidden Dangers of Reading the Novel

How often have I seen girls not twelve years old as hungry for a story or novel as they should be for their dinners! A sickly sentimentalism is thus formed, and their minds are sullied with impure desires.

Every fashionable young lady must, of course, read every new novel, though nearly all of them contain exceptionable allusions, perhaps delicately covered over with a thin gauze of fashionable refinement; yet, on that very account, the more objectionable. If this work contained one improper allusion to their ten, many of those fastidious ladies who now eagerly devour the vulgarities of Dumas, and the double entendres of Bulwer, and even converse with gentlemen about their contents, would discountenance or condemn it as improper.

Shame on novel-reading women, for they cannot have pure minds or unsullied feelings, but
Cupid and the beaux, and waking of dreams
of love, are fast consuming their health and
virtue.

Theater-Going and Other Vices: Paths to Impurity

 Theaters and theatrical dancing inflame the passions and are "the wide gate" of "the broad road" of moral impurity.

Fashionable music is another, especially the verses set to it, being mostly lovesick ditties, or sentimental odes, breathing this tender passion in its most melting and bewitching strains. Improper prints often do immense injury in this respect, as do also balls, parties, annuals, newspaper articles, exceptional works, etc.

No other source contributes so much to sexual immorality as obscene literature. The mass of stories published in the great weeklies and the cheap novels are mischievous. When the devil determines to take charge of a young soul, he often employs a very ingenious method. He slyly hands a little novel filled with "voluptuous forms," "reclining on bosoms," "languishing eyes," etc.

It is painful to see strong intelligent men and youths reading bad books, or feasting their eyes on filthy pictures, for the practice is sure to affect their personal purity. Impressions will be left which cannot fail to breed a legion of impure thoughts, and in many instances, criminal deeds.

Thousands of elevator boys, clerks, students, traveling men, and others patronize the questionable literature counter to an alarming extent.

For years there has been a great craze after the nude in art and the realistic in literature. Many art galleries abound in pictures and statuary which cannot fail to fan the fires of

sensualism, unless the thoughts of the visitor are trained to the strictest purity. Why should artists and sculptors persist in shocking the finer sensibilities of old and young of both sexes by crowding upon their view representations of naked human forms in attitudes of luxurious abandon? Public taste may demand it. But let those who have the power endeavor to reform public taste.

Many of our young men lack moral principle. They cannot look upon a beautiful girl with a pure heart and pure thoughts. Men who have no self-control will find life a failure, both in a social and in a business sense. The world despises an insignificant person who lacks backbone and character. Stand upon your manhood and womanhood; honor your convictions, and dare to do right.

Man is the brain, but woman is the heart of humanity; he its judgment, she its feeling; he its strength, she its grace, ornament, and solace. Even the understanding of the best woman seems to work mainly through her affections. And thus, though man may direct the intellect, woman cultivates the feelings, which mainly determine the character. While he fills the memory, she occupies the heart. She makes us love what he can make us only believe, and it is chiefly through her that we are enabled to arrive at virtue.

To be a woman is something more than to live eighteen or twenty years; something more than to grow to the physical stature of women; something more than to wear flounces, exhibit dry goods, sport jewelry, catch the gaze of lewd-eyed men; something more than to be a belle, a wife, or a mother. Put all these qualifications together and they do but little toward making a true woman.

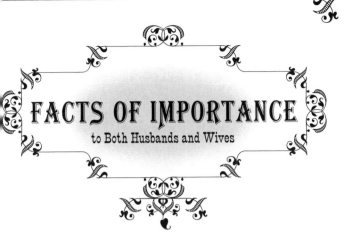

FACTS OF IMPORTANCE

to Both Husbands and Wives

Marriage purifies the complexion, removes blotches from the skin, invigorates the body, fills up the tones of the voice, gives elasticity and firmness to the step, and brings health and contentment to old age. If the prudent avoid marriage, while the reckless marry, the inferior members will tend to supplant the better members of society.

An Understanding of Female Attractiveness

The proportions of the perfect human figure are strictly mathematical. The whole figure is six times the length of the foot. Whether the form be slender or plump, this rule holds good. Any deviation from it is a departure from the highest beauty of proportion.

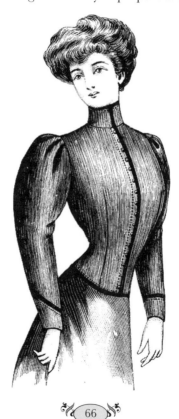

Beauty's Demands

To beautify the hair, keep the head clean, the pores of the skin open, and the whole circulatory system in a healthy condition, and you will have no need of bear's grease (alias hog's lard). Where there is a tendency in the hair to fall off on account of the weakness or sluggishness of the circulation, or an unhealthy state of the skin, cold water and friction with a tolerably stiff brush are probably the best remedial agents.

A woman at thirty, well courted and well married, looks five or ten years younger than a woman of the same age unhappily married. Old maids and bachelors always look older than they are. A flirting widow always looks younger than an old maid of like age.

The old maid is like any other woman. She has faults necessarily, though not those commonly conceived of. She is often plump, pretty, amiable, interesting, intellectual, cultured, warm-hearted, and benevolent, and she has ardent friends of both sexes. She usually has a sentimental, romantic, frequently sad and pathetic past, of which she does not speak unless in the sacredness of intimacy.

Dissipated single men, professional libertines, and married men who are immoderate often pay the penalty of their violations of the laws of nature by losing their vital power. Impotence from mental and moral causes often takes place. Persons of highly nervous organization may suffer incapacity in their sexual organs. The remedy for these difficulties is rest and change of occupation.

Coffee drank excessively causes a debilitating effect upon the sexual organs. The moderate use of coffee can be recommended, yet an excessive habit of drinking very strong coffee will sometimes wholly destroy vitality.

Hysteria in Women

DEFINITION. *A functional disorder of the nervous system characterized by disturbance of the reason, will, imagination, and emotions, with sometimes convulsive attacks that resemble epilepsy.*

SYMPTOMS. *Fits of laughter and tears without apparent cause; emotions easily excited; mind often melancholy and depressed; tenderness along the spine; disturbances of digestion, with hysterical convulsions and other nervous phenomena.*

HOME TREATMENT. *Some healthy and pleasant employment should be urged upon women afflicted with this disease. Men are also subject to it, though not so frequently. Avoid excessive fatigue and mental worry; also stimulants and opiates. Plenty of good food and fresh air will do more good than drugs.*

Practical Rules for Bathing

No person should think for a moment that they can be popular in society without regular bathing. A bath should be taken at least once a week, and if the feet perspire they should be washed several times a week, as the case may require.

1. Bathe at least once a week all over, thoroughly. No one can preserve his health by neglecting personal cleanliness. Remember, "Cleanliness is akin to Godliness."

2. Only mild soap should be used in bathing the body.

3. Wipe quickly and dry the body thoroughly with a moderately coarse towel. Rub the skin vigorously.

4. Many people have contracted severe and fatal diseases by neglecting to take proper care of the body after bathing.

5. If you get up a good reaction by thorough rubbing in a mild temperature, the effect is always good.

6. Never go into a cold room, or allow cold air to enter the room, until you are dressed.

7. Bathing in cold rooms and in cold water is positively injurious, unless the person possesses a very strong and vigorous constitution, and then there is great danger of laying the foundation of some serious disease.

8. Never bathe within two hours after eating. It injures digestion.

9. Never bathe when the body or mind is much exhausted. It is liable to check the healthful circulation.

10. A good time for bathing is just before retiring. The morning hour is a good time also, if a warm room and warm water can be secured.

11. Never bathe a fresh wound or broken skin with cold water; the wound absorbs water and causes swelling and irritation.

12. A person not robust should be very careful in bathing; great care should be exercised to avoid any chilling effects.

A young man who allows his mind to dwell upon the vision of nude women will soon become a victim of ruinous passion, and either fall under the influence of lewd women or resort to self-abuse.

Non-Completed Intercourse

Withdrawal before the emission occurs is injurious to both parties. The soiling of the conjugal bed by the shameful maneuvers is to be deplored.

It is a well-known fact that any man who desires to excel and retain his excellence as an accurate shot, an oarsman, a pedestrian, a pugilist, a first-class cricketer, bicyclist, student, artist, or literary man, must abstain from self-pollution and fornication. Thousands of school boys and students lose their positions in the class,

and are plucked at the time of their examination by reason of failure of memory, through lack of nerve and vital force, caused mainly by draining the physical frame of the seed which is the vigor of the life.

The Law of Magnetism

When two bodies are brought into contact with each other, the weak must naturally draw from the strong until both have become equal. And as long as this equality exists, there will be perfect harmony between individuals, because of the reciprocation which exists in their nature.

But if one should gain the advantage of the other in magnetic attraction, the chances are that through the law of development, or what has been termed the "Survival of the Fittest," the stronger will rob the weaker until one becomes robust and healthy, while the other grows weaker and weaker day by day.

This frequently occurs with children sleeping together, also between husband and wife. A well person should never sleep with an invalid if he desires to keep his health unimpaired, for the weak will take from the strong, until the strong becomes the weak and the weak the strong. Many a husband has died from a lingering disease which saved his wife from an early grave. He took the disease from his wife because he was the stronger, and she became better and he perished.

It is not always wise that husband and wife should sleep together, nor that children—whose temperament does not harmonize—should be compelled to sleep in the same bed. By the same law it is wrong for the young to sleep with old persons. Some have slept in the same bed with persons, when in the morning they have gotten up seemingly more tired than when they went to bed. At other times with different persons, they have lain awake two-thirds of the night in pleasant conversation and have gotten up in the morning without scarcely realizing that they had been to sleep at all, yet have felt perfectly rested and refreshed.

Determining Disposition and Character from Physical Characteristics

Tall persons have high heads and are aspiring, aim high, and seek conspicuousness, while short ones have flat heads and seek the lower forms of worldly pleasures. Tall persons are rarely mean, though often grasping; but very penurious persons are often broad built.

Small persons generally have exquisite mentalities, yet less power—the more precious the article, the smaller the package in which it is done up—while great men are rarely dwarfs, though great size often coexists with sluggishness.

When scientifically observed, the variety of other bodily and personal characteristics reveal many other truths.

LARGE NOSES.—Bonaparte chose large-nosed men for his generals, and the opinion prevails that large noses indicate long heads and strong minds. Not that great noses cause great minds, but that the motive or powerful temperament causes both.

FLAT NOSES.—Flat noses indicate flatness of mind and character by indicating a poor, low organic structure.

BROAD NOSES.—Broad noses indicate large passageways to the lungs, and this, large lungs and vital organs, and this, great strength of constitution and hearty animal passions along with selfishness—for broad noses, broad shoulders, broad heads, and large animal organs go together. But when the nose is narrow at the base, the nostrils are small, because the lungs are small and need but small avenues for air; and this indicates a predisposition to consumptive complaints, along with an active brain and nervous system, and a passionate fondness for literary pursuits.

SHARP NOSES.—Sharp noses indicate a quick, clear, penetrating, searching, knowing, sagacious mind, and also a scold; indicate warmth of love, hate, generosity, moral sentiment—indeed, positiveness in everything.

BLUNT NOSES.—Blunt noses indicate and accompany obtuse intellects and perceptions, sluggish feelings, and a soulless character.

ROMAN NOSES.—The Roman nose indicates a martial spirit, love of debate, resistance, and strong passions, while hollow, pug noses indicate a tame, easy, inert, sly character, and straight, finely formed Grecian noses indicate harmonious characters. Seek their acquaintance.

Their Expression of Character

Those who give a tame and loose hand, and shake lightly, have a cold if not heartless and selfish disposition, rarely sacrificing much for others; are probably conservatives; and lack warmth and soul. But those who grasp firmly, and shake heartily, have a corresponding whole-souledness of character, are hospitable, and will sacrifice business to friends; while those who bow low when they shake hands, add deference to friendship and are easily led, for good or bad, by friends.

Disposition and Character Determined by the Walk

AWKWARD.—Those whose motions are awkward yet easy, possess much efficiency and positiveness of character, yet lack polish; and just in proportion as they become refined in mind will their movements be correspondingly improved. A short and quick step indicates a brisk and active but rather contracted mind, whereas those who take long steps generally have long heads; yet if the step is slow, they will make comparatively little progress, while those whose step is long and quick will accomplish proportionately much and pass most of their competitors on the highway of life.

A DRAGGING STEP.—Those who sluff or drag their heels drag and drawl in everything; while those who walk with a springing, bouncing step abound in mental snap and spring. Those whose walk is mincing, affected, and artificial, rarely, if ever, accomplish much; whereas those who walk carelessly, that is, naturally, are just what they appear to be and put on nothing for outside show.

THE DIFFERENT MODES OF WALKING.—In short, every individual has his own peculiar mode of moving, which exactly accords with his mental character; so that, as far as you can see such modes, you can decipher such outlines of character.

NOTE: The following is said to be a correct posture for walking. Head erect—not too rigid—chin in, shoulders back. Permit no unnecessary motion about the thighs. Do not lean over to one side in walking, standing, or sitting; the practice is not only ungraceful, but it is deforming and therefore unhealthful.

Disposition and Character Ascertained from Laughing

LAUGHTER EXPRESSIVE OF CHARACTER.—
Laughter is very expressive of character. Those
who laugh very heartily
have much cordiality and
whole-souledness of char-
acter, except that those
who laugh heartily at
trifles have much feeling,
yet little sense. Those
whose giggles are rapid
but light have much
intensity of feeling, yet lack power; whereas
those who combine rapidity with force in laugh-
ing combine them in character.

VULGAR LAUGH.—Vulgar persons always laugh
vulgarly, and refined persons show refinement in their laugh. Those who ha, ha right
out, unreservedly, have no cunning and are
openhearted in everything; while those who
suppress laughter, and try to control their coun-
tenances in it, are more or less secretive. Those
who laugh with their mouths closed are non-
committal; while those who throw it wide open
are unguarded and unequivocal in character.

On Standard Characteristics of the Bastard

Illegitimates or Bastards are generally lively, sprightly, witty, frolicksome, knowing, quiet of perception, apt to learn, full of passion, quick-tempered, impulsive throughout, hasty, indiscreet, and given to excesses, yet they abound in good feeling and are well calculated to enjoy life, though in general sadly deficient moral elements. They are commonly wanting in moral balance, or else delinquent in some important moral aspect; nor would they have ever been born unless this had been the case, for the time being at least with their parents.

SUPPRESSED LAUGHTER.—Those who, suppressing laughter for a while, burst forth volcano-like, have strong characteristics, but are well-governed, yet violent when they give way to their feelings. Then there is the intellectual laugh, the love laugh, the horselaugh, the philoprogenitive laugh, the friendly laugh, and many other kinds of laughs, each indicative of corresponding mental developments.

Determining Disposition and Character by the Mouth and Eyes

DIFFERENT FORMS OF MOUTHS.—Every mouth differs from every other and indicates a coincident character. Large mouths express a corresponding quantity of mentality, while small ones indicate a lesser amount. A coarsely formed mouth indicates power, while one finely formed indicates exquisite susceptibilities. Hence small, delicately formed mouths indicate only common minds, with very fine feelings and much perfection of character.

CHARACTERISTICS.—Whenever the muscles about the mouth are distinct, the character is correspondingly positive, and the reverse. Those who open their mouths wide and frequently, thereby evince an open soul, while closed mouths, unless to hide deformed teeth, are proportionately secretive.

EYES.—Those who keep their eyes half shut are peek-a-boos and eavesdroppers.

EXPRESSIONS OF THE EYE.—The mere expression of the eye conveys precise ideas of the existing and predominant states of the mentality and physiology. As long as the constitution

remains unimpaired, the eye is clear and bright, but becomes languid and soulless in proportion as the brain has been enfeebled. Wild, erratic persons have a half-crazed expression of eye, while calmness, benignancy, intelligence, purity, sweetness, love, lasciviousness, anger, and all the other mental affections express themselves quite as distinctly by the eye as voice, or any other mode.

COLOR OF THE EYES.— Some inherit fineness from one parent, and coarseness from the other, while the color of the eye generally corresponds with that of the skin and expresses character. Light eyes indicate warmth of feeling, and dark eyes power.

Discerning Secretive Dispositions

If a lady naturally inclines to high-necked dresses and collars, she will keep her secrets to herself if she has any.

In courtship or love she is an uncertainty, as she will not reveal sentiments of her heart. The secretive girl, however, usually makes a good house-keeper and rarely gets mixed into neighborhood difficulties. As a wife she will not be the most affectionate, nor will she trouble her husband with many of her trials or difficulties.

Those who keep their coats but up and fancy high-necked and closed dresses, etc., are equally non-communicative, but those who like open, free, flowing garments are equally openhearted and communicative.

If a man wears his hat well down on the forehead, shading the eyes more or less, he will always keep his own counsel. He will not confide a secret, and if criminally inclined, will be a very dangerous character.

Determining Disposition and Character from the Hair

DIFFERENT COLORS.—Coarseness and fineness of texture in nature indicate coarse and fine-grained feelings and characters, and since black signifies power, and red ardor, therefore coarse black hair and skin signify great power of character of some kind, along with considerable tendency to the sensual; yet fine black hair and skin indicate strength of character, along with purity and goodness.

COARSE HAIR.—Coarse black hair and skin, and coarse red hair and whiskers, indicate powerful animal passions, together with corresponding strength of character; while fine or light, or auburn hair, indicates quick susceptibilities, together with refinement and good taste.

FINE HAIR.—Fine dark or brown hair indicates the combination of exquisite susceptibilities with great strength of character, while auburn hair, with a florid countenance, indicates the highest order of sentiment and intensity of feeling, along with corresponding purity of character, combined with the highest capacities for enjoyment and suffering.

CURLY HAIR.—Curly hair or beard indicates a crisp, excitable, and variable disposition, and much diversity of character—now blowing hot, now cold—along with intense love and hate, gushing, glowing emotions, brilliancy, and variety of talent. So look out for ringlets; they betoken April weather—treat them gently, lovingly, and you will have the brightest, clearest sunshine, and the sweetest balmiest breezes.

STRAIGHT HAIR.—Straight, even, smooth, and glossy hair indicates strength, harmony, and evenness of character, and hearty, whole-souled affections, as well as a clear head and superior talents; while straight, stiff, black hair and beard indicate a coarse, strong, rigid, straightforward character.

ABUNDANCE OF HAIR.—Abundance of hair and beard signifies virility and a great amount of character; while a thin beard signifies sterility and a thinly settled upper story, with rooms to let, so that the beard is very significant of character.

RED HAIR.—Fiery red hair indicates a quick and fiery disposition. Persons with such hair generally have intense feelings—love and hate intensely—yet treat them kindly, and you have the warmest friends, but ruffle them, and you raise a hurricane on short notice. This is doubly true of auburn curls. It takes but little kindness, however, to produce a calm and render them as fair as a summer morning. Redheaded people in general are not given to hold a grudge. They are generally of a very forgiving disposition.

The Dangers of Beauty

Thousands of the most beautiful women are destitute of common sense and common humanity. No gift from heaven is so general and so widely abused by woman as the gift of beauty. In about nine cases in ten it makes her silly, senseless, thoughtless, giddy, vain, proud, frivolous, selfish, low, and mean.

I think I have seen more girls spoiled by beauty than by any other one thing. "She is beautiful, and she knows it," is as much as to say that she is spoiled. A beautiful girl is very likely to believe she was made to be looked at; and so she sets herself up for a show at every window, in every door, on every corner of the street, in every company at which opportunity offers for an exhibition of herself. Beauty is shallow—only skin deep; fleeting—only for a few years' reign; dangerous—tempting to vanity and lightness of mind; deceitful—dazzling often to bewilder; weak—reigning only to ruin; gross—leading often to sensual pleasure.

A Miscellania of Important Facts

The perfect corset is one which possesses just

that degree of rigidity which will prevent it from wrinkling, but will at the same time allow freedom in the bending and twisting of the body. Corsets boned with whalebone, horn, or steel are necessarily stiff, rigid, and uncomfortable. After a few days' wear the bones or steels become bent and set in position, or, as more frequently happens, they break and cause injury or discomfort to the wearer.

There are many children born healthy and vigorous who destroy the full vigor of their generative organs in youth by self-abuse, and if they survive and marry, their children will have small bones, small frames, and sickly constitutions. It is therefore not strange that instinct should lead women to admire men not touched with these symptoms of physical debility.

Marks and deformities are all transmissible from parents to offspring, equally with diseases and peculiar proclivities. Among such blemishes may be mentioned moles, hair-lips, deficient or supernumerary fingers, toes, and other characteristics. It is also asserted that dogs and cats that have accidentally lost their tails bring forth young similarly deformed. Blumenbach tells of a man who had lost his little finger, having children with the same deformity.

Children born of overworked mothers are liable to be a dwarfed and puny race.

Pregnant mothers should avoid thinking of ugly people—or those marked by any deformity or disease—and avoid injury, fright, and disease of any kind. They should also avoid ungraceful position and awkward attitude, but cultivate grace and beauty in themselves. They should avoid difficulty with neighbors or other trouble. Low spirits, violent passions, irritability, and frivolity in the pregnant woman leave indelible marks on the unborn child.

After the birth of the baby, the mother should be kept perfectly quiet for the first twenty-four hours and not be allowed to talk or see anyone except her nearest relations, however well she may seem. She should not get out of bed for ten days or two weeks, nor sit up in bed for nine days. The more care taken of her at this time, the more rapid will be her recovery when she does get about. She should go up and down stairs slowly, carefully, and as

seldom as possible for six weeks. She should
not stand more than is unavoidable during
that time, but sit with her feet up and lie down
when she has time to rest. She should not work
a sewing machine with a treadle for at least six
weeks.

Dr. Dio Lewis says: "Some of the most common effects of sexual excess are backache,
lassitude, giddiness, dimness of sight, noises
in the ears, numbness of the fingers, and
paralysis. The drain is universal, but the more
sensitive organs and tissues suffer most. So the
nervous system gives way and continues the
principal sufferer throughout. A large part of
the premature loss of sight and hearing, diz-
ziness, numbness and pricking in the hands
and feet, and other kindred developments are
justly chargeable to unbridled venery. Not

unfrequently you see men whose head or back or nerve testifies of such reckless expenditure."

Dr. Lewis further observes:

A man who is badly dressed feels chilly, sweaty, and prickly. He stammers and does not always tell the truth. He means to, perhaps, but he can't. He is half distracted about his pantaloons, which are much too short, and are constantly hitching up; or his frayed jacket and crumpled linen harrow his soul, and quite unman him.

A young girl, and especially one of a light and airy style of beauty, should never wear gems. A simple flower in her hair or on her bosom is all that good taste will permit. When jewels or other ornaments are worn, they should be placed where you desire the eye of the spectator to rest, leaving the parts to which you do not want attention called as plain and negative as possible. There is no surer sign of vulgarity than a profusion of heavy jewelry carried about upon the person.

During "the monthly periods" violent exercise is injurious; iced drinks and acid beverages are improper; and bathing in the sea, and bathing the feet in cold water, and cold

How To Remove Superfluous Hair

Sulphuret of Arsenic, one ounce

Quicklime, one ounce

Prepared Lard, one ounce

White Wax, one ounce

Melt the wax, add the lard. When nearly cold, stir in the other ingredients. Apply to the superfluous hair, allowing it to remain on from five to ten minutes; use a table knife to shave off the hair; then wash with soap and warm water.

baths are dangerous; indeed, at such times as these, no risks should be run, and no experiments should, for the moment, be permitted, otherwise serious consequences will, in all probability, ensue.

A wound made by thrusting a dagger or other oblong instrument into the flesh is best treated, if no artery has been severed, by applying lint scraped from a linen cloth, which serves as an obstruction, allowing and assisting coagulation. Meanwhile cold water should be applied to the parts adjoining the wound.

A man who is helplessly intoxicated may almost immediately restore the faculties and powers of locomotion by taking half a teaspoonful of chloride of ammonium in a goblet of water. A wineglassful of strong vinegar will have the same effect and is frequently resorted to by drunken soldiers.